Discover other cultures

Items should be returned on or before the last date shown below. Items not already requested by other borrowers may be renewed in person, in writing or by telephone. To renew, please quote the number on the barcode label. To renew online a PIN is required. This can be requested at your local library.
Renew online @ **www.dublincitypubliclibraries.ie**
Fines charged for overdue items will include postage incurred in recovery. Damage to or loss of items will be charged to the borrower.

Leabharlanna Poiblí Chathair Bhaile Átha Cliath
Dublin City Public Libraries

Dublin City
Baile Átha Cliath

Date Due	Date Due	Date Due
0 1 APR 2019		

About this book

People make baskets all over the world in a huge variety of different shapes, sizes, materials and decorations. In this book, we have tried to show as many styles of basket as possible.

We begin with the main techniques used in traditional basketwork: coiling, sewing, weaving and plaiting. Baskets can also be made using a looped and knotted mesh – a technique that developed from the knotting of fishing nets. We also look at some of the more unusual materials that can be used to make baskets, such as twigs, wire and wood.

Basket-making techniques can also be used to make other items like hats, decorations and even a toy vehicle (see page 26).

Most of the steps used to make the baskets are very easy to follow, but where you see this sign ask for help from an adult.

Baskets are light, versatile containers that we use for hundreds of everyday purposes. Yet they can be so much more than that. The skills that are used to create traditional baskets often make the baskets works of art in their own right. Many people are now collecting different examples of basketwork, before the traditional skills of basket-making disappear.

Display your basket collection

We hope that this book will inspire you to begin your own basket or basketwork collection. On pages 28 and 29 you will find some ideas for displaying your baskets. At your school or youth club, you could put together a display or make baskets to sell at a local fund-raising or charity event.

This edition 2005

First published as *World Crafts: Baskets*
Design and illustration © Franklin Watts 1997, 2005
Text © Meryl Doney 1997, 2005

Franklin Watts
96 Leonard Street, London EC2A 4XD

Franklin Watts Australia
Level 17/207 Kent Street, Sydney, NSW 2000

ISBN: 0 7496 6324 3

Dewey Decimal Classification 745.54

Series editor: Sarah Snashall
Editor: Jane Walker
Design: Visual Image
Cover design: Jonathan Hair
Artwork: Ruth Levy
Photography: Peter Millard

With special thanks to Myra McDonnell, advisor and basket-maker, and thanks to Rosy Dyer and Matilda Harrison.

A CIP catalogue record for this book is available from the British Library

Printed in Dubai

Contents

Useful and beautiful

The art of making objects from tree bark and plant fibres can be traced all the way back to prehistoric times. Yet because baskets are made from materials that perish quite quickly, only a few examples have been found. However, impressions left in clay as well as wooden carvings from ancient civilizations tell us something about the earliest baskets. This wooden figure of a servant girl from Ancient Egypt is carrying a basket full of loaves.

Basketwork is especially important in tropical areas of the world, such as Equatorial Africa, South America and South-East Asia. In these climates, creepers, bark, bamboo and leaves grow quickly. They are a cheap and natural resource for making everyday items from thatched houses, boats and furniture to nets, clothes, hats – and, of course, baskets. This bus in the Philippines (below right) is loaded with baskets for market. In Ancient Egypt and in Peru, people were even buried in basket-like coffins.

Baskets are not only containers. They have been used for more serious purposes. The Dayak people of Kalimantan, on the island of Borneo, used to behead their enemies and present the heads to their chief in baskets like the one above! The baskets were then hung in the trees as a warning to the Dayak's enemies (see page 20). Baskets can also feature in religious ceremonies. In Bangladesh, a flower basket called a *phuler shaji* is used for a *puja*, or special celebration. In some parts of the country a special basket symbolizes Lakshmi, the Hindu goddess of fortune.

The baskets in this book are made by a wide variety of peoples around the world. They demonstrate that simple household objects, when made with love, can also be beautiful.

Your own basket-making kit

Most of the baskets in this book are very simple to make and do not require expensive raw materials. Here is a list of the basic tools and equipment that you may need.

hammer • hand drill • scissors • needle-nosed pliers • craft knife • metal ruler • brushes • paint • varnish • strong glue •

masking tape • card • paper • pen • pencil • needle and thread • newspaper to work on • card to cut on

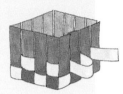

Raw materials

Most basket weavers use materials that are available locally. These are some of the plants and fibres that are most often used around the world. You may like to experiment with whatever materials you can easily find, from the leaves of pot plants like yucca to saplings from local trees. (Always ask an adult before removing any plant material.)

bamboo A plant of the grass family. It grows in tropical and other warm areas. Bamboo is quick growing and very strong.

banana Fibres are used from the leaves and bark of the banana palm tree.

jute An annual plant that grows up to four metres tall. Basket-makers use the fibres from its stems. Most jute comes from Bangladesh.

raffia Fibre is stripped from the upper surface of young raffia palm leaves in West Africa.

rattan or cane Thorny, climbing palms or creepers that cling to other trees in the rainforests of southern and South-East Asia.

savannah straw or grass The stems of long grasses that grow on the plains of Africa.

sisal Fibres are taken from the succulent leaves of this plant, which comes from Central and South America.

Coils and stitches

Coiling is one of the simplest methods of making bowls and baskets. This loosely coiled waste-paper basket from China (right) shows how straw or the stems of grasses can be twisted into a bundle. They are then sewn together using thin strips of cane. Decoration has been added by wrapping the straw bundles in raffia leaves. Some of them have been dyed blue. The flat basket from Ethiopia (below right) shows how the basketwork begins at a central point and spirals outwards and upwards to make the shape required.

It is possible to create wonderful designs using coiling. Natural colours and special stitching decorate the bowl from Zambia (below centre, back). A mixture of coloured dyes has been used by women in Swaziland to make the sisal baskets shown below left (see page 28).

The lids for the little raffia-sewn baskets from Colombia (below right) have also been made by coiling.

Make a trinket basket

This basket is oblong in shape but you can make a round basket by folding over only 1 cm at the start. The stitches can be close together or spread apart, but they should all be the same.

You will need: hank (coil) of raffia • needle • ruler • scissors • small button

1 Divide raffia into bunches of 10 strands each. Thread needle with long strand of raffia.

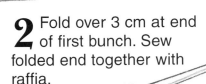

2 Fold over 3 cm at end of first bunch. Sew folded end together with raffia.

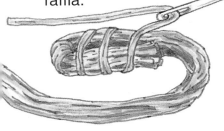

3 Coil bunch around oblong shape and sew across two coils. Keep work flat between your fingers. Continue until base measures 10 x 8 cm.

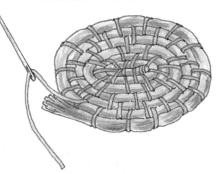

4 Lay next coil on top of last one. Sew in place.

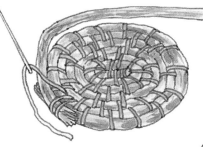

Continue coiling upwards until sides of basket measure 5 cm. To finish, cut bunch to a point and sew end down neatly. Finish sewing on the inside.

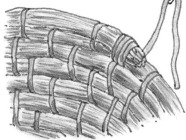

5 To make lid, repeat steps 1–3.

6 Sew lid to basket rim with two sets of stitches to form a hinge. Knot raffia on inside.

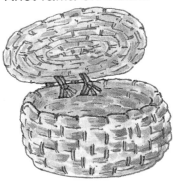

7 Plait three pieces of raffia to form a loop. Push loop through front coil of lid and sew ends down. Sew button on front of basket.

Sewn by hand

Here is another hand-sewn method of making baskets. The bowl-shaped basket from Bangladesh (below centre) is made from rattan cane. The thorns and leaves have been stripped from the flexible creeper stem. The stem is then dried, washed and bleached. It is coiled to form the basket, but the sewing that holds it together passes through each strand and cannot be seen. The decorations and a base made from split canes are added at the end of the process.

The eight-sided basket (below right) comes from China. It is sewn in the same way as the rattan one, but the canes are hollow and cannot form curves. They have been bent into shape and sewn tightly with thread.

Stiff grass stems are sewn together to make the basket from Burkina Faso (below left). It is then finished by adding split stems in a spiral around the outside, sewn in a decorative pattern. The edge is neatened with a leather strip.

The fine stems of the savannah grass that grows on the African plains are sewn together to make this oblong basket (below) from Burkina Faso. Coloured plastic strips are used as decoration and edging. Cowrie shells are sewn onto the base to form feet.

Make a straw pot

You will need: stiff card • a food tin (a tin of baked beans, soup or fruit is suitable) • pencil • scissors • 71 21-cm paper straws • masking tape • ruler • glue • needle • thread • thin ribbon • thin paper strips • paper strip, 3 x 40 cm

1 Stand tin on card. Draw around base. Cut out card circle.

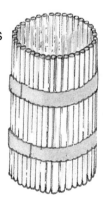

2 Lay straws next to one another on a flat surface. Tape together.

3 Lift straws and roll into a tube. Tape ends together.

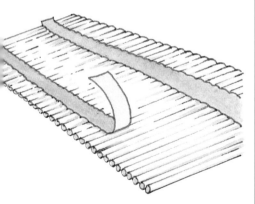

4 Bend bottom 6 cm of straws inwards to form base.

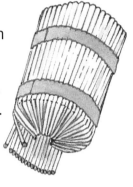

5 Push tin down inside tube to flatten base. Glue card circle to base. When dry, remove tin.

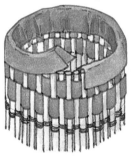

6 Use needle to weave thread around tube at top and near base. Remove masking tape.

7 Weave ribbon and other materials around pot for decoration. Push thin paper strips between straws and overlap ends on inside.

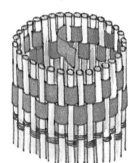

8 Fold 3-cm paper strip over rim and glue.

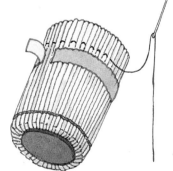

Wickerwork

The best-known method of basket-making is called stake-and-strand weaving. It is started by creating a series of upright strands. These are sometimes set in a wooden base as in this tray (below right). However, the strands are usually laid across each other and woven from the base upwards, as the waste-paper basket (below left) shows. The horizontal strands are woven in and out of the upright ones, in the same way that cloth is woven. This basket weaver in the Philippines is using flat strips of cane to make a linen basket.

In cooler climates, where rattan creepers and canes do not grow naturally, traditional basket-making material often comes from the willow tree. If the young tree is continually cut back, it grows long, pliable shoots called osiers. These are cut and stripped and their bark is peeled off. The baskets are sometimes called 'wickerwork' from *vikker*, the Swedish word for willow. The base of this traditional English wicker waste-paper basket (below, far left) is woven around six strands of willow. Other strands are then added in before the sides of the basket are woven.

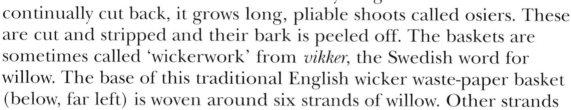

Make a cane basket

Cane can be bought in various thicknesses – nos. 6 and 8 are middle weights that can be used for uprights and weaving. Plastic cane is also available and does not need to be soaked first. Once you learn this technique you can make any size of basket. Vary the spaces by weaving every third upright or by weaving with two canes at a time. To add some decoration, thread beads onto the uprights between weaving rows.

You will need: a hank of no. 6 centre cane • scissors • ruler • washing-up bowl • water • small basket base, 12.5-cm diameter with 19 holes

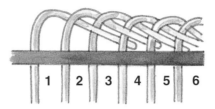

1 Cut 19 25-cm canes. Push 5 cm of each cane through holes in base. Soak remaining canes in water.

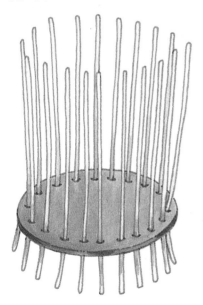

2 For base, bend cane 1 to right. Weave behind cane 2 and in front of cane 3. Tuck behind cane 4. Repeat process with cane 2. Continue until all canes are woven.

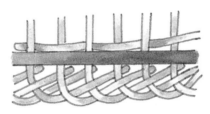

3 Turn basket over. Tuck end of one long (pre-soaked) cane behind cane 1. Weave in and out of alternate uprights around basket.

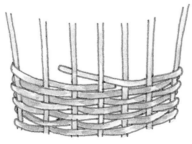

4 When cane is used up, tuck end inside. To begin new cane, tuck end behind 2nd cane before last woven one.

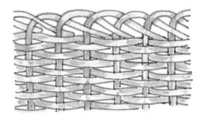

5 Continue until basket reaches required height. To make the edge, soak the cane ends. Repeat directions in step 2. Cut off canes on inside of basket.

PHILIPPINES, BANGLADESH, ITALY & UGANDA

From houses to handbags

Since earliest times, wood, cane and grasses have been used to make flat-woven panels for many different domestic uses. In countries like the Philippines, where bamboo canes are easily available, whole houses like this one on the right are constructed from bamboo. The strong stems form the frame, and the walls are woven from split sections of cane. The leaves are used to thatch the roof. Similar skills are also used to make household goods like this bamboo tray from Bangladesh (below right).

Flat-woven grass mats can be adapted to make all kinds of containers. Two examples of this method are this pencil case from the Philippines and the clutch bag from Italy (below centre).

The basket tray from Uganda (below left) is formed from a large flat-woven panel. The edges are bound with a chequered pattern of dyed leaves. The pattern across the middle of the tray has been painted onto individual sections after the weaving has been completed.

Make a clutch bag

You can make a bag from any soft weave material. Tablemats are an ideal material. A beach mat will provide enough weave for several bags. You could make some for your friends.

You will need: card, 54 x 33 cm • metal ruler • pencil • craft knife • fabric, 60 x 39 cm • piece cut from woven beach mat, 54 x 33 cm • scissors • glue • needle • thread • ribbon, 1 m long

1 Draw two lines across card, one 19 cm and the other 38 cm from right-hand edge. Use metal ruler and craft knife to score lightly along lines.

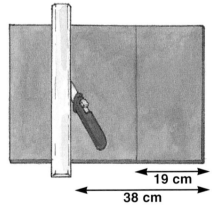

19 cm
38 cm

2 Place fabric face down. Lay card on top, with scored side down. Lay woven mat on top.

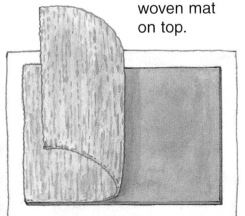

3 Fold fabric corners inwards at right-angles. Snip off point. Turn over 1 cm of fabric on all four sides and tack in place.

4 Fold fabric in again and glue to mat. Remove tacking stiches.

5 Fold fabric, card and mat into three along scored lines. Sew along two 19-cm sides, to make pocket.

6 Fold ribbon at 30 cm. Sew folded end to front flap. Tie around bag to secure.

Unusual materials

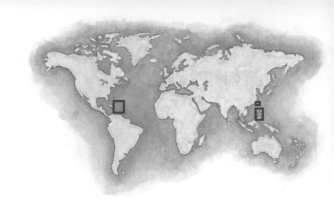

Here are some good examples of the ways in which people use local materials to make their baskets. The round basket from Taiwan (left) is woven using the traditional stake-and-strand method (see page 10). Flexible vines have been used for the base and rim, and knobbly vine twigs form the sides.

This plant basket (below right), with its twisty vine handle, is made by the villagers of Quezon Island in the Philippines. The vines are quite large but flexible and have been wound around a frame made from sticks. The villagers now make objects out of vine stems instead of timber. Logging has been made illegal in many areas to protect the forests, and so the vines provide these people with an alternative source of income.

This unusual-looking basket below is made in the West Indies. Its maker has used the natural curve of the outer husks of the coconut to form the shape. The slices of husk are sewn together with vines.

Weave a honeysuckle basket

Almost any twigs can be made into a basket. If you have a garden or live near woodland, try finding flexible plant or tree stems. Wisteria, honeysuckle and vines are ideal. (Make sure you ask an adult before cutting anything.)

You could introduce colour by weaving thin strips of plastic bag or string into your finished basket. This basket is made from honeysuckle cuttings with the bark left on.

You will need: bunch of bendy twigs • ruler • block of wood with four headless nails forming a square, 10 x 10 cm • coloured string or raffia • large needle

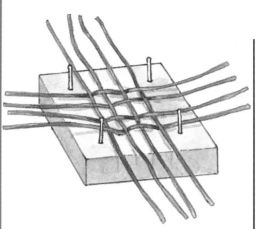

5 Weave more twigs across the basket to strengthen and fill in spaces.

3 Repeat with three more twigs, passing under and over different twigs each time to form rough weave.

6 To finish edge, bend twigs sideways and weave into basket.

1 Strip twigs of leaves (and bark if you wish). Pick out eight pieces about 36 cm long.

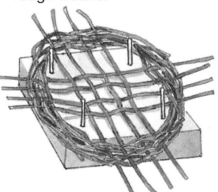

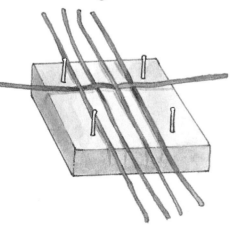

4 Weave thinner and longer twigs around twigs outside nails. Remove from wood support.

7 Thread coloured string or raffia into needle. Sew edge at intervals to secure twigs.

2 Lay four twigs across wood between nails. Lay next twig across others at right angles. Pass twig under and over four twigs.

Twisting and twining

Twining is another form of stake-and-strand weaving. It involves using at least two horizontal strands at a time, and giving them a twist between each vertical stake. This method is usually used when the stake is made from a flexible material rather than a rigid one. This loose-weave shopping bag (below, far right) was bought in the Netherlands. If you look closely, you will see that the strands are twisted together. The brightly coloured toy basket above comes from Ecuador.

The flexibility and strength of twined baskets, like this one from the Bolgatang district of northern Ghana (below, back right), make them very good shopping carriers. These baskets are made from dyed savannah straw, and the handles are bound with leather. They are used for carrying market produce, for storage or for collecting locusts. Similar round twined baskets are made in Kenya (below centre). They are woven from natural and dyed sisal and are called *kiondo* bags. It takes a woman weaver one week to complete each bag. The men add the finishing touches of leather binding, purse and straps.

Twining can also be used to make fine baskets like these grain winnowing baskets (left) from Zimbabwe. They are made from *ilala* palm fibre.

Make a shopping basket

This basket is made from rug backing canvas. Look carefully at this material and you will see that the horizontal threads have been twisted once between the vertical strands. This is an example of twining.

You will need: piece of rug backing canvas, 55 x 100 cm • scissors • ruler • large books (telephone directories are ideal) • coloured string • large-eyed needle • sewing pins • card, 14 x 22 cm

1 To make handles, cut strip 24 x 55 cm from one short side of canvas. Cut strip in half and trim both halves to 40 cm long.

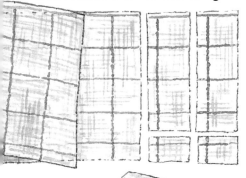

Fold each strip in three, lengthways.

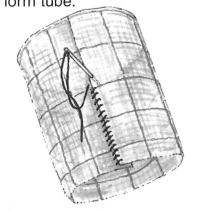

2 Sew ends of large canvas together to form tube.

3 Make stack of books that measures about 14 x 22 cm. Slip books into canvas tube, leaving gap of 10 cm between books and one end.

4 Fold short sides of tube in like a parcel. Fold top flap down, bottom flap up. Sew bottom of tube together with string. Remove books.

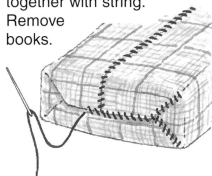

5 Fold top edge over twice. Tuck inside basket.

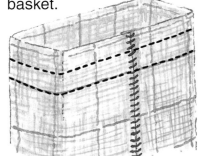

6 Sew along length of each handle. Pin handle ends to inside top edges of basket. Sew in place.

Wedge card in bottom of basket.

17

Stakes and strands

Stake-and-strand weaving can be done with flat strips of material. This is a traditional form of weaving in colder, northern climates, especially the Scandinavian countries. Thin strips of wood are cut from pine or birch trees and woven into hampers like this one from Sweden (below centre, back).

Strips of wood have been used to make the traditional English flower basket, or trug (above). The strips are cut to shape, heated and bent. They are then held in place with nails. Bark has been left on the wood of the rim and on the handle of the basket for decoration.

The taller-handled basket (below right) is a traditional shape from Finland. The tray-shaped basket below uses the same technique but is made from birch bark. This forms a softer strip which makes a more flexible basket.

The strawberry punnet is a good example of packaging made from natural materials. Very thin strips of wood have been stapled together to make the punnet.

Make a paper basket

Once you have learned this technique, you can make many different shapes of basket. Try making the lidded box, which consists of two baskets, one slightly bigger than the other.

You will need: two large sheets of different-coloured card • ruler • pencil • scissors • masking tape • strong glue

1 Cut one sheet of card into eight strips, 4 x 60 cm. Mark each strip 22 cm from each end. Cut second sheet into three strips, 4 x 75 cm.

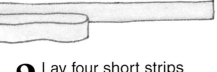

2 Lay four short strips next to one another. Tape ends together to stop movement. Weave fifth short strip at right angles across the four strips. Repeat with next three strips.

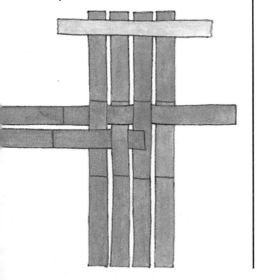

3 Remove tape. Bend all four sides upwards at marks. Weave first long strip around bottom of basket. Bend card at corners. Overlap ends on the inside. Weave three rows.

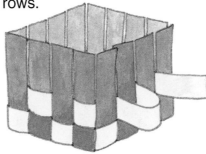

4 To finish top edge, bend ends inside and outside alternately. Glue down.

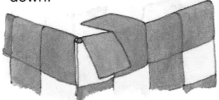

5 For handle, cut one strip, 42 x 2 cm, in first colour of card and two strips of same size in second colour. Overlap strips and glue together. Glue inside basket.

India, Indonesia, Colombia & China

Plaiting patterns

Plaiting is a more complicated form of weaving. There is no upright stake, but two or more strands are woven together in a plaiting movement. This gives the weaver the flexibility to produce colourful patterns. The black and cream woven rattle from India (below centre) shows this method of plaiting clearly.

The red and black bamboo basket shown right is made by the Dayak people of Kalimantan, Indonesia. The 'wave' pattern is very old and is said to symbolize fertility and solidarity. It is formed by using flat bamboo strips that are painted on one side with coloured resins. The strips are woven over and under one another to form the shapes. These baskets were originally used to carry the severed heads of the Dayak's enemies (see page 4)!

The Cundu basket (below right) is made by the people living on the Pacific coast of Colombia in South America. It is plaited with a very loose weave which allows the basket to be squashed into any shape. Cundu baskets are mostly used for carrying fish and fruit. Plaited split-cane work forms the sides of this elaborate Chinese lunch box (below left). The box is made from painted and carved bamboo. It has two baskets, a tray and a lid that are stacked, one on top of the other, to hold the picnic.

Make a gift box

To make the panels of this box we have used pre-woven split cane. This is sold in craft shops for repairing the cane seats of chairs. You could use any woven material, such as a table mat. Alternatively, you could weave your own panels from very thin strips of card, following the instructions on page 19.

You will need: firm card, cut into the following pieces: two side pieces, 20 x 15 cm; two end pieces, 10 x 15 cm; one base, 10 x 20 cm; one lid, 21 x 11 cm; two strips for lid sides, 3 x 21 cm; two strips for lid ends, 3 x 11 cm • scissors • metal ruler • pencil • craft knife • wooden board • sticky tape • glue • 0.5 metres of chair cane • coloured paper • paint • brush • varnish

1 Measure 2.5 cm from edges of side, end and lid pieces. Draw rectangle on each. Place card on board and use craft knife and ruler to cut out rectangles. Cut across corners of lid.

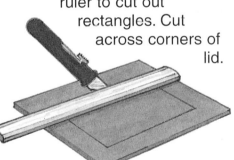

2 Assemble box. Glue joins and tape together. Leave to dry. Remove tape.

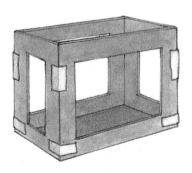

3 Glue chair cane to sheet of coloured paper. Using cut-out rectangles as guides, cut cane panels 2 cm larger all

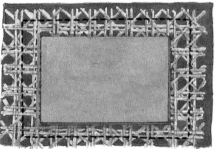

round. Glue panels across holes on inside of box.

4 To make lid, glue together side and end pieces. Tape and leave to dry. Add four strips of lid top, gluing corners at slight angle. Glue cane panel into lid.

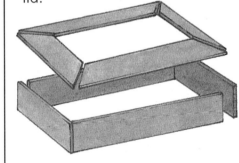

5 Paint box. Coat with varnish for a shiny finish.

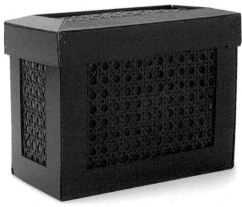

Knotting and knitting

The skill of making fishing nets from knotted string is also used to make baskets. Such baskets are light and flexible, but they can hold bulky and odd-shaped things. They take up very little space when empty. The shopping bag (below centre) is made from jute fibres that are twisted and knotted together. This one is made by a women's cooperative in Bangladesh.

Soft baskets can also be made using knitting or crochet stitches. The shoulder bag (below left) is made in China. The string is formed from two reeds twisted together. It is not particularly strong until it is knotted together. This method is called Tunisian crochet.

The women of the Wahgi people of Papua New Guinea make bags called *bilums* (below right). They use a method called knotless netting or looping. The bags are made using a single thread so that they cannot run or ladder. Early *bilums* were stitched from natural fibres using a bone needle and a pandanus leaf as a gauge to keep the stitches apart. Today, Wahgi women use acrylic thread with umbrella-spoke needles and plastic parcel strapping for the gauge.

The large striped basket from India (top right) is made from knotted plastic strips. It is designed to hook over bicycle handlebars.

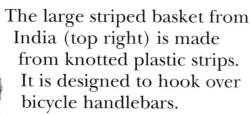

Knit you own string bag

To make your work loose enough, you will need very big knitting needles. You can make your own needles from two 30-cm lengths of 15-mm dowel rod. Use a craft knife to shave the ends into points.

You will need: two balls of different-coloured string • pair of fat knitting needles • scissors • sewing needle • ruler

1 To cast on, knot a loop in string and slip onto left needle. Push the right needle through the loop from front to back.

2 With your right finger, loop string over right needle.

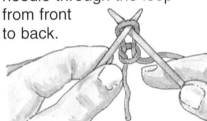

3 Pull string through loop and slip it onto left needle. Repeat using this new loop. Continue until you have 40 stitches on the left needle.

4 To knit, push right needle into first stitch. With right finger, loop string around left needle.

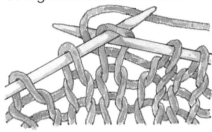

5 Pull string through stitch and slip it onto right needle. Knit 20 rows. Change colour every two rows. Cut string and tie second colour to cut end.

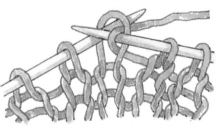

6 To cast off, knit two stitches. Push the left needle through the first stitch and lift it over the second.

Knit another stitch and repeat casting-off process to end. Knot last stitch.

7 Fold knitting in half. Sew along bottom edge and up side.

8 Cut 12 lengths of string, 60 cm long. Knot together in three groups of four and plait.

9 Thread plait through the top stitches of bag. Knot in centre. Pull out loops at sides for handles.

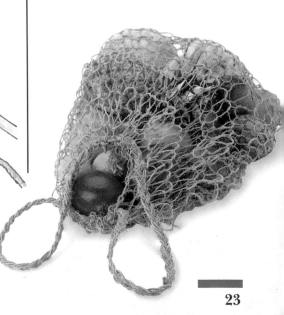

SOUTH AFRICA, POLAND & SWEDEN

Baskets from wire

Wire is a completely different material for making baskets. It is strong but it can be shaped fairly easily. You can use wire to make good, rigid mesh baskets for many different purposes. It is stronger than natural fibres and can be used outdoors in colder climates. We also use plastic-covered wire baskets inside refrigerators and freezers.

This ingenious use of telephone wire to make a strong, colourful basket (above) comes from South Africa. Modern telephone cables are made up of plastic-coated wires in many colours. Here, the wires are woven together in a spiral design that moves from the centre outwards.

The uncoated wire baskets (below) are made in Poland. The designs are simple, yet the added curves make them fun. Thick wires form the basic shape, and thinner wires bind them together. The soap dish comes from Sweden. It is decorated with a heart, a traditional symbol in European folk art. Originally the heart was a symbol of God's love, and it was only after the Victorian period that it became associated with people's love for each other. This style of decoration was brought to North America by the early settlers from Europe. It became known as Pennsylvania Dutch.

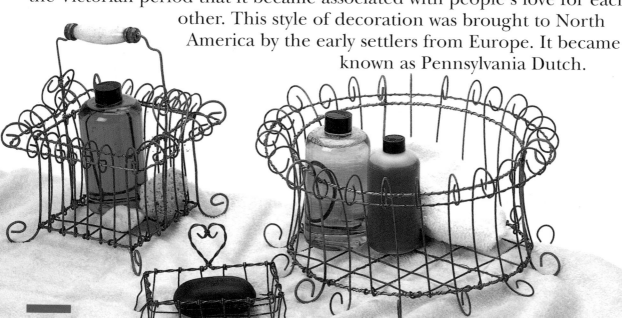

Make a soap dish

This method of twisting thin wire makes a strong strand that is still easily bent. It looks attractive, too.

You will need: roll of 0.8-mm copper wire • ruler • wire cutters • small metal eyelet or hook • hand drill • two pairs of needle-nosed pliers • felt-tip pen

1 To form a length of twisted wire, measure double the length you need and add 10 cm. Fold in half and ask someone to hold the ends.

2 Open up ring of eyelet. Insert straight end into the chuck of a hand drill. Loop wire over eyelet, hold it taut and turn drill handle until wire is evenly twisted.

3 Twist one length of wire to measure 46 cm, four lengths to 13 cm and two to 19 cm. Mark longest wire with felt-tip pen at 5, 5, 8, 10, 8, 5 and 5 cm. Mark 2.5 cm from both ends of six remaining lengths of wire.

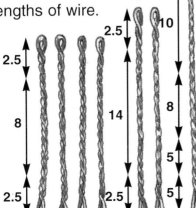

4 Begin by making front of dish. Grip longest wire with pliers at marks and bend into a rectangle. Twist last 5 cm together and form into heart shape.

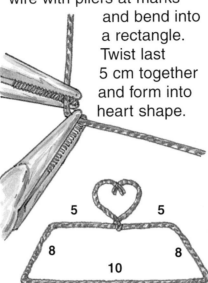

5 On all six shorter lengths of wire, bend both 2.5-cm ends upwards and form hooks at both ends.

6 Loop four shorter lengths at intervals over sides of dish. Twist round and squeeze to secure in place.

7 On two longer lengths, form two loops to make feet.

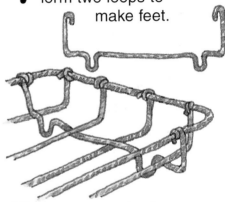

Weave across shorter lengths. Loop over each end. Twist and secure.

Not quite baskets!

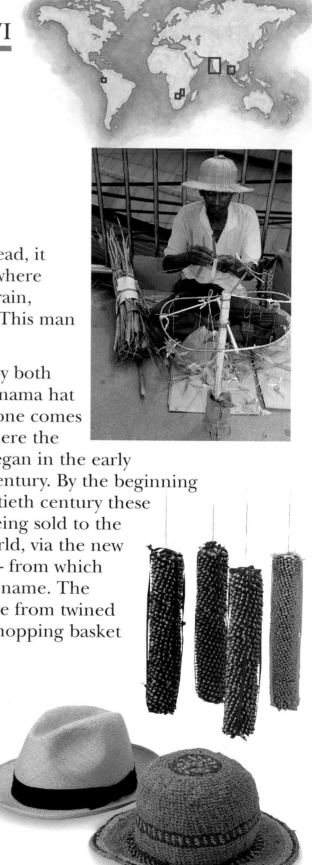

If you turn a basket over and put it on your head, it makes a fine hat! In countries like Thailand, where people work in the open air in sunshine and rain, basketwork hats are an important protection. This man is wearing one as he works.

In South America, hats of all kinds are worn by both men and women. The finest of these is the Panama hat (bottom left). This one comes from Ecuador, where the trade in hats began in the early nineteenth century. By the beginning of the twentieth century these hats were being sold to the rest of the world, via the new Panama Canal – from which they gained their name. The round hat (bottom right) is made in Zimbabwe from twined fibres. It is made by the same method as the shopping basket on page 16.

All kinds of decorations can be made by weaving. These dyed palm leaf streamers (middle right) come from southern India. The jeep is made in Malawi. It shows quite a different use for traditional basket-making. The wheels are coiled grasses sewn with palm leaves, and the axles are made from cane. Palm leaves have been sewn around strips of cane to form the body.

Make a raffia jeep

You will need: a piece of card, 6 x 12 cm • two pieces of card, 1.5 x 14.5 cm • pencil • ruler • scissors • craft knife • metal ruler • base of large matchbox, 11.5 x 6 cm • raffia • large, sharp needle • rope washing line • plastic straw • glue • thin, green garden cane

1 Mark 6 x 12-cm card at 2, 2, 2 and 2 cm. Cut one 4 x 6-cm piece for bonnet and two 4 x 6-cm pieces for seats. Use craft knife to score seats along 2-cm lines.

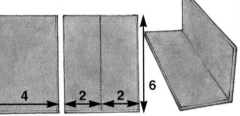

2 Mark and score both 14.5-cm strips (for mudguards) at 3.5, 2.5, 2, 2.5 and 3 cm.

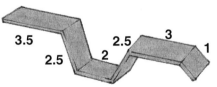

3 Sew through base and around each side of matchbox with raffia.

4 Sew along both sides of card seats. Cover mudguards by oversewing ends and wrapping raffia along length. Repeat with bonnet, sewing through the centre.

5 Make wheels by coiling washing line until each coil measures 4 cm across (see page 7).

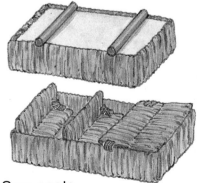

6 Cut straw into two 6-cm lengths. Glue to base of jeep.

Sew seats and bonnet in place with two raffia stitches.

7 Sew mudguards to sides of jeep in three places as shown.

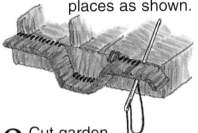

8 Cut garden cane into two 10-cm pieces. Push wheel onto one end. Thread through back straw. Add second wheel. Repeat for front wheels.

Colours and designs

Colour and decoration are very important in basketwork. It is these two elements that give each country's baskets their distinctive character. The materials themselves can be used to make the decoration, as in the canework basket from South-East Asia (bottom right).

Another effect can be created by embroidering on a finished basket with wools or dyed raffia. The fabric sides of the basket from Poland (bottom left) have been embroidered in wool with a vase of brightly coloured, exotic flowers.

Natural materials can also be dyed to add to the decoration. The striking design on this *inkangara* basket from Rwanda (right) is added after a plain base has been woven from raffia bamboo. Fine papyrus stems, some of which have been dyed black, are then stitched in place over the top. The lid is made in the same way, and the papyrus is sewn around it in a spiral.

These baskets from Swaziland (above right) show how dyed sisal can be used to make an infinite number of patterns (see page 6). The women who make them take their designs from nature and everyday life, for example fish, stars or flights of birds. Fine baskets like these are often collected as much for their beauty as for their usefulness. Collectors like to show them off by hanging them on the wall as a display.

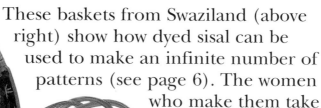

Display your basket collection

When you have made several baskets, or started a collection of your own, you may like to display them together.

You will need: a collection of baskets • paper • pencil • hammer • small-headed panel pins or picture hook and pins • large needle • length of raffia

1 Find a suitable wall space or display board. Make sure that you have permission to use it.

2 Lay out your baskets on the floor and position them to make an attractive display. Make a sketch of the display to guide you as you work.

3 If you have permission and the baskets are lightweight, you may be able to nail them directly onto the wall or board. Push a panel tack with a small head between the woven or coiled strands to one side of the base area. Use a light hammer to knock the tack straight into the surface.

4 If you are using a painted or papered wall, you may need to use a picture hook. Tack the hook into the wall in the correct position.

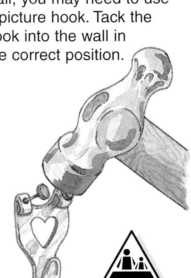

5 Thread a needle with raffia. Sew into the basket from the back, on one side of the base area. Sew out again and tie ends together to form a loop.

6 Place loop over picture hook. Continue to hang baskets until you have displayed your collection.

Useful information

United Kingdom

Websites

www.asiasociety.org/arts/
baskets/material.html
*(website about Japanese
bamboo baskets)*

www.britishbaskets.co.uk/
history.htm

www.crossroadstrade.com/
baskets.php
(all about baskets from Panama)

http://eaglechief.com/ECSplash.
asp
*(see authentic Native American
baskets, antique and modern)*

www.kibseycraft.co.uk
*(all about a traditional basket-
maker in Wales)*

www.sussexbaskets.co.uk

Museums

Pitt Rivers Museum
South Parks Road
Oxford OX1 3PP
Tel. 01865 270927
www.prm.ox.ac.uk/australia.html
*(Australian baskets on display,
more information on the website)*

The British Museum
Great Russell Street
London WC1B 3DG
Tel. 020 7323 8000
www.thebritishmuseum.ac.uk
(various baskets on display)

Australia

Websites

www.amonline.net.au/
anthropology/collections/pacific/
pacific05.htm
*(traditional basket-weaving
in Vanuatu)*

Museums

South Australian Museum
North Terrace
Adelaide 5000
Tel. 61 8 8207 7500
http://www.samuseum.sa.gov.au/
aacg/speakingland/story18/18_
story.htm
*(information about Aboriginal
basket-making)*

Every effort has been made by
the Publisher to ensure that these
websites are suitable for children,
and contain no inappropriate or
offensive material. However, due
to the nature of the Internet, it is
impossible to guarantee that the
contents of these sites will not be
altered. We strongly advise that
Internet access is supervised by
a responsible adult.

Glossary

creeper A plant which cannot support itself. It grows along the ground or up trees.

fertility The ability to produce a good harvest of crops. Also refers to the ability of animals, including humans, to produce young.

fibre A thin thread of plant material. Also refers to the threads that make up a fabric or material such as wool or cotton.

flexible Can be bent in any direction.

gauge A device used to measure a standard thickness or fineness.

husk The dry, outer covering of a fruit or seed.

ingenious Clever or inventive.

mesh Strands that are placed at right angles to each other to form a net or sieve.

pandanus A plant that grows in Papua New Guinea. Local women use its leaves to separate their stitches when knitting *bilum* bags (see page 22).

perish To spoil or become useless with age.

resin A kind of gum that is made from the sap of plants and trees.

sapling A young tree or a shoot from a tree root.

savannah A grassy plain in a tropical or subtropical region.

stake and strand A method of weaving that uses upright stakes and horizontal strands.

succulent Juicy. Also the name of a kind of plant that stores water in its leaves or stem.

symbolize To use a picture or object to represent something else. For example, a dove symbolizes peace.

twining Twisting two strands together.

wicker Saplings from the willow tree. It is used in basket-making.

winnowing A method of removing the dry, outer leaves, or chaff, from grain. The whole grain is thrown up in the air, and the wind blows away the chaff.

Index

Additional photographs:

page 4: (top) © British Museum, (bottom) OXFAM;
page 10 (top): OXFAM/J. Hartley; page 12 (top):
OXFAM/ N. Regalado; page 22 (bottom right):
Michael O'Hanlon; page 26 (top): Christine
Osborne Pictures; page 28 (top): OXFAM.